EXHIBIT DESIGN 5

EXHIBIT

DESIGN

5

ROBERT B. KONIKOW

PBC

Library of Applied Design

An Imprint of

PBC INTERNATIONAL, INC. ◆ NEW YORK

Distributor to the book trade in the United States and Canada:

Rizzoli International Publications Inc.
300 Park Avenue South
New York, NY 10010

Distributor to the art trade in the United States and Canada:

PBC International, Inc.
One School Street
Glen Cove, NY 11542
1-800-527-2826
Fax 516-676-2738

Distributor throughout the rest of the world:

Hearst Books International
1350 Avenue of the Americas
New York, NY 10019

Library of Congress Cataloging-in-Publication Data

Konikow, Robert B.
    Exhibit design 5 / by Robert B. Konikow.
        p.   cm.
    Includes index.
    ISBN 0-86636-149-9
    1. Exhibitions.   I. Title.   II. Title: Exhibit design five.
T396.5.K654   1992
659.1'52--dc20   92-3520
                                                  CIP

CAVEAT—Information in this text is believed accurate, and will
pose no problem for the student or casual reader.
However, the author was often constrained by information
contained in signed release forms, information that could
have been in error or not included at all. Any misinformation
(or lack of information) is the result of failure in these
attestations. The author has done whatever is possible to
insure accuracy.

Printed in Hong Kong

10 9 8 7 6 5 4 3 2 1

Contents

Foreword

I like to think of trade shows as portable shopping centers that draw an exclusive customer base which is decidedly interested in the products offered for sale. The setting is a great equalizer for large, mid-sized and small companies. All have parallel openings to reach the same buyers.

Today, the exposition industry is one of the most cost effective marketing tools available to promote and sell products and services. As we evolve into a truly global marketplace, opportunities to bring new buyers and sellers together gain even more significance in our marketing plans.

Designing a display seems deceptively simple on the surface. Upon closer inspection we find that exhibit designers and producers are challenged to translate a company's marketing objectives into a positive visual impact and to create a successful sales environment. The blending of the two is critical, because we all know a beautiful, empty booth produces no sales results.

Design considerations include such things as allowance for visitor traffic flow and proper staffing mixes, effortless execution of administrative tasks in front of the potential buyers, and product demonstrations/presentations, all often within a relatively confined space.

Additionally, the builder must engineer this "portable store" so that it can be set up and dismantled multiple times in a short time span, usually by strangers to the company and its objectives.

Trade Show Bureau studies indicate that size is the most important factor in creating "memorability" of a display. However, lest we get too caught up in capacity, we must also look at the content and the "fashionability" of the design. Like apparel and home furnishings, displays follow their own fashion trends. Some designs are classics, some are more trendy. And, with the variety and availability of more and more textiles and fabrics, the exhibit designer can be even more creative.

Robert Konikow is a long-time, respected observer and contributor to the exposition industry. This collection represents the best of the best in exhibit design and layout.

As you look through the wonderful presentation of exhibit designs to follow in **Exhibit Design 5**, I hope you will keep some of the thoughts I am offering in mind. An exhibit design is only as good as the sum of its parts—the visual impact, meeting the marketing needs and addressing the human factors in the selling environment.

E. JANE LORIMER, *President*
Trade Show Bureau

Preface

When I started on the first of this series of books on exhibit design, back in 1983, neither the publisher nor I was sure that there would be enough interest in having a book like this, or enough available material, to continue the series. As its title indicates, this is the fifth such volume to be released. The series is now an accepted tool of the industry, used as a showcase, as an inspirational source, and as an aid to better communication.

Perhaps those designers and producers who are represented in this volume would have some curiosity about how the 200 or so exhibits that are included have been selected. And those who are not included may have even more curiosity.

The book starts with a broad invitation to the exhibit community to submit examples of their work for consideration. An invitation, along with an entry form, was sent to every exhibit designer and producer on our mailing list in the United States and Canada. This encompasses somewhere between 1,350 and 1,400 companies. In addition, a press release was sent to every publication that reaches members of the exhibit industry, announcing the start of work on the new book and inviting readers to request an entry form from the publisher. The same release is sent to every exhibit industry trade association, in as many countries around the world as we have information on.

Gradually, the flat packets with pictures and entry forms come trickling in. At first, I may get only one package at a time, every couple of days. Then they come more rapidly and in greater quantity. The peak, this year, was reached on the actual deadline, October 1, 1991, when there were 27 separate deliveries to my office! And, of course, about a week before the deadline, the calls requesting an extension of time start, and I find the explanations for the request interesting. I wonder, for example, why so many companies find that their best work is first shown the week before the deadline, and the pictures haven't yet been processed. Or that the entry form, when it was received in July, was given to a responsible staff member. However, she quit in September, and it turned up in her desk just today! But I believe that most exhibit companies have got into the habit of doing nothing on a project until the deadline is impending. And then they pay overtime to get the photos printed, and send the material by air!

As the entries arrived, I checked them in, and entered them in a special HyperCard file I set up on my Macintosh. At this time, I assigned them to the chapter or chapters indicated by the submitter, and counted the number and type of graphic materials submitted with the entry. At this point there was no attempt to evaluate the entries. Everything that I received, as long as the entry form was legible, was logged in.

At the end of the deadline day, there was a pile of entries in front of me, all of which were logged in during the next few days. When that was done, I could start making my selection of those that should be in the book. I started with a couple of the specialized chapters, one on museum exhibits and the other on exhibits outside of the trade show. These two, which are somewhat special, were followed by the other six, tackling those with the fewest entries first.

In the meantime, additional entries kept dribbling in, and were opened and logged in. They were assigned to their appropriate chapters, and if that had been completed, the new entries waited until, if necessary, I had to reexamine that chapter.

Some entries needed only a quick examination to be discarded. First of all, the photography had to be good. Both the publisher and I are very conscious of the over-all appearance of the finished volume, and of the high standards of the industry. The pictures must be sharp and of good color, and they must show enough of the exhibit to be meaningful to the reader. It is frustrating to examine an entry, read the submitter's description, and then to find that the photo falls short and is unusable.

And, of course, the picture should present the interesting features of the exhibit. One would think this would be obvious, but too often, the entry form would describe what the designer felt was unique about this exhibit. The photos, however, failed to include this special feature, and this often made the entry seem like a run-of-the-mill design.

Since one of the objectives of the book is to present a cross-section of the best design being done everywhere, we imposed a condition that helped to broaden the book's basis. We set up a rule-of-thumb that said that no more than two exhibits in a single chapter could be from a single exhibit company, and no more than five in the entire volume. This kept a company which had submitted a lot of

entries from overwhelming those which had sent in only one or two, but it was interpreted loosely, so that no outstanding exhibit, as I saw it, was automatically ruled out.

A number of entrants had checked off more than one box on the entry form. This was understandable and expected. It is no conflict when the entry form has checkmarks in both "over 4,000 square feet" and "multi-level." Such an exhibit could be placed in either category, and I selected the category, depending partly on how well the multi-level features were illustrated, and influenced to some extent by my need to fill out certain chapters.

Once I had decided I wanted to include a specific entry, I wrote the descriptive material. While this is based, in general, on the information that was given on the entry form, it was subject to my own evaluation of the material and of the supporting illustrations. The credits, however, are taken directly from the entry form. Whenever a name was included, without company affiliation, as the designer, we assumed that he/she was a staff member of the company listed as the exhibit producer, but if another affiliation were included, that was listed as given. When the same company was listed as both designer and producer, we simply made the designation read "designer/producer."

Once the selection had been made, and the test material written, the packet was shipped to the publisher. Some entries had only a single picture, and others had as many as two dozen! The final selection of photographs was made by the designer of the book,

who chose those to be used on the basis of what would make the most attractive and informative lay-out on the page.

I would like to thank all those who submitted entries, and I wish we had enough space to use everything of value that was sent in. I am sure that another editor would have made a somewhat different selection, but I am equally sure that perhaps as much as 75 percent of his selections would have been mine, too. There are standards of design, but they are intuitive rather than empirical.

One must remember that trade show exhibits are not purchased because they rank high in esthetics. Their objective is to help the exhibitor achieve a particular marketing goal, and this is not easy for an outsider to measure. One of the reasons for this is that it is not easy for an insider to define. Too often, I am afraid, the procedure is done backwards. The results are measured after a show is over, and then the goals are written to make the project seem like an effective one.

In making the selections for this book, we had to rely on what the entry blanks told us, and how the photos struck us. But as I leafed through the pile of photos that had been accepted, I felt that the standards were pretty high, and that this was an adequate representation of the best work being done today. I hope that you will find this selection a good reflection of what we see on the show floor, and that it continues to be a useful guide to what is going on within this changing industry. Your comments would be appreciated.

ROBERT B. KONIKOW

CHAPTER **1**

THE SMALL EXHIBIT

<400 ft² (37 m²)

EXHIBITOR
Accent Exhibits Designs & Displays
DESIGNER
Judy Blumberg, Richard Strittmaster
PRODUCER
Accent Exhibits Designs & Displays
Baltimore, MD

This bright and attractive exhibit was originally designed for use as a rental unit, but when it was used as the designer/producer's own exhibit, it offered such a pleasant background, that it became psychologically difficult to offer it for rent.

EXHIBITOR
Federal Aviation Administration
DESIGNER
Kat Mallette, The Gerard Company
PRODUCER
Adler Display Inc.
Baltimore, MD

This 20′ exhibit is constructed of Nimlock's Nimlink panels. The 4 × 8′ panel in the center randomly flashes the nine regions of the FAA.

EXHIBITOR
Axxess/Oregon Scientific
DESIGNER
Greg Arhart
PRODUCER
All West Display
Portland, OR

To introduce a new information retrieval system, called "axxess," the exhibitor wanted a clean, elegant, and professional design. The exhibit is asymmetrical, with a private conference area and a signage tower surrounded by three brightly-lit, double-sided demo units.

EXHIBITOR
Mendix Corp.
DESIGNER
Daniel Burk
PRODUCER
General Exhibits

Actual samples of the product, accompanied by photography, form an eye-catching design for this attractive back wall. Edge-lit plexi shelves add scattered bright notes.

EXHIBITOR
Color & Design Exhibits Inc./Intex
International Exhibits
DESIGNER/PRODUCER
Color & Design Exhibits Inc.
Portland, OR

The 16' high triangle was placed along the diagonal of a $20 \times 20'$ space, with one side serving as the back wall of the mother company, and the other for its systems division, Intex.

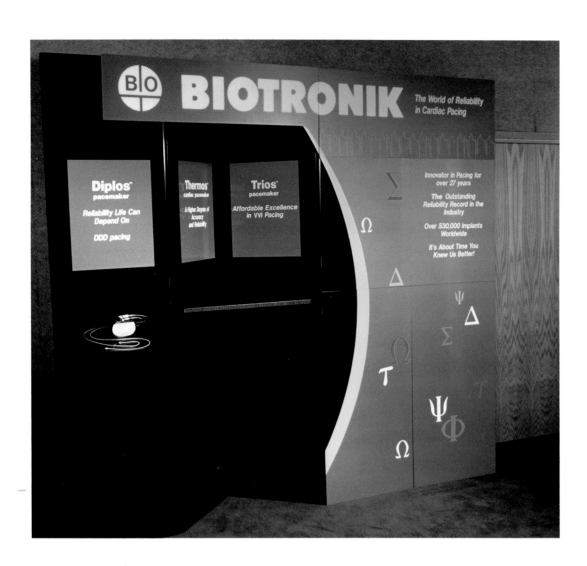

EXHIBITOR
Biotronik
DESIGNER/PRODUCER
Color & Design Exhibits Inc.
Portland, OR

To meet the exhibitor's needs for easy transportability and professional image, the designer turned to Fastpack II panels, five of which were used. The set-up time is less than ten minutes, and the entire display is shipped in three lightweight, easy-to-transport cases.

EXHIBITOR
GE Appliances
DESIGNER
Richard Thurman
PRODUCER
Deckel & Moneypenny
Louisville, KY

To demonstrate GE's new range, three full-size appliances were installed, each in its own complete kitchen.

CONTINUED

EXHIBITOR
Teklogix Inc.
DESIGNER
Stephen G. Roach
PRODUCER
Dell Displays Inc.
Elk Grove Village, IL

This special configuration of Mo-bilite panels gives the exhibitor an out of the ordinary look for major shows, and yet it breaks down into a 20′ in-line structure, or into two separate 10′ booths.

EXHIBITOR
Pharmacia
DESIGNER
Charles P. Koch
PRODUCER
Ad-Ex International
Cincinnati, OH

Separate demo stations face the aisles in this simple island booth. The identification tower can be in-stalled at different heights, going as high as 16′ where permitted.

19

EXHIBITOR
Beech-Nut
DESIGNER
John Edmunds
PRODUCER
Design South
Atlanta, GA

Because Beech-Nut was promoting baby food and wanted the environment to be "fun," it agreed to an exhibit which was reminiscent of a child's playroom. The design incorporated children's building blocks on a giant scale, using a variety of shapes and forms. Bold, primary colors were chosen, not only for their playfulness and ability to attract attention, but also for their use in the product packaging.

EXHIBITOR
Viskase
DESIGNER
Ernest E. Errigo
PRODUCER
Dimensional Studios Inc.
Runnemede, NJ

This 20′ linear exhibit calls attention to itself with dramatic large back-lit transparencies, each supported by a similar panel containing descriptive copy that expands on the theme suggested by the photo.

EXHIBITOR
Obron Atlantic
DESIGNER
John Kolin
PRODUCER
Exhibit Builders Inc.
Cleveland, OH

Simple design, clean shapes, and an uncluttered appearance allowed the very subtle product, metallic pigments, to become highly visible.

EXHIBITOR
Wako Diagnostics
DESIGNER
Michael Edwards
PRODUCER
Exhibitgroup Atlanta
Atlanta, GA

Identification was easy with the illuminated cubical sign seeming to float above the exhibit on the diagonal truss structure. The truss also held spotlights that illuminated the demonstrations at workstations.

EXHIBITOR
Computone
DESIGNER
Mark S. Burns
PRODUCER
Exhibitgroup Atlanta
Atlanta, GA

While this exhibit gave the appearance of solidity, its internal aluminum structure, held together with a specially-designed locking mechanism, actually made it light in weight and easy to set up rapidly.

EXHIBITOR
Four Seasons Hotels & Resorts
DESIGNER
Tom Yurkin; Wilson & Assoc.
PRODUCER
Freeman Exhibit Co.
Dallas, TX

The extraordinary use of elaborate materials, including burled wood, verde marble, and fine furnishings brought the luxurious feeling of a Four Seasons hotel to the show floor.

EXHIBITOR
Fairmont Hotels
DESIGNER
Tom Yurkin; Wilson & Assoc.
PRODUCER
Freeman Exhibit Co.
Dallas, TX

The circular header, with its suggestion of Washington's Capitol Dome, ties in the newest addition to the Fairmont Group and gives the feeling of being in other properties of the chain.

EXHIBITOR
Radisson Hotels International
DESIGNER
Rod Folland, Mark Bendickson
PRODUCER
Haas Exhibit Marketing
Minneapolis, MN

This modular display shows off the exhibitor's properties through the use of large back-lit transparencies. The maximum use is made of a limited amount of floor space.

EXHIBITOR
Texaco
DESIGNER
David Eurton, Sr.
PRODUCER
Giltspur/Chicago
Chicago, IL

The red connecting nodes on the white iso-frame canopy makes this structure appear to be designed exclusively for Texaco. This $20 \times 20'$ configuration is actually part of a larger $20 \times 90'$ corporate exhibit.

EXHIBITOR
Medtox Laboratories Inc.
DESIGNER
Dick Giffin
PRODUCER
Haas Exhibit Marketing
Minneapolis, MN
Exponents
San Diego, CA

This is evidence that a modular system can achieve high design capabilities, and in a very tight time frame. While the panels were being finished, the graphics were produced elsewhere, to meet the other components on the floor.

EXHIBITOR
Arandell-Schmidt
DESIGNER
G.P. Lyons
PRODUCER
Hartwig Exhibitions
Milwaukee, WI

With nothing cluttering the aisle, this exhibit lends itself to good traffic flow. There is lots of space along the back wall to display sample product.

EXHIBITOR
H-Window
DESIGNER
Bill Kneeland, Darrold Johnson
PRODUCER
Haas Exhibit Marketing
Minneapolis, MN
Exponents
San Diego, CA

Any window made by the exhibitor can be held in place between a pair of hexagonal pylons. These same pylons are made available to dealers for use in their showrooms.

EXHIBITOR
Anixter Bros. Inc.
DESIGNER
Howard A. Jacobs
PRODUCER
Howard Displays Inc.
Chicago, IL

This stand, only $2 \times 5'$, was developed to introduce a new product. It had to fit into an existing island display, but without taking up very much space. This unit shows off the item itself, as well as eight transparencies, a two-sided sign, storage and literature cases.

EXHIBITOR
Farm Credit Bank
DESIGNER
James L. Colbert
PRODUCER
John Oldham Studios Inc.
Wethersfield, CT

This simple design is given dignity by its use of natural oak and copper.

EXHIBITOR
Everfresh Inc.
DESIGNER/PRODUCER
Kitzing Inc.
Chicago, IL

Demonstrating the exhibitor's approach to the environment, this display was constructed of recyclable products. No lacquer was used on the wood, and parquet flooring was used instead of carpet.

EXHIBITOR
Young Dental Mfg.
DESIGNER
David Hurt
PRODUCER
Pingel Displays
St. Louis, MO

The Nimlink system from Nimlok was what was needed to furnish a regular 10′ exhibit that could also be set up as three tabletop displays.

EXHIBITOR
FactSet Data Systems
DESIGNER
McMillan Group
Wilton, CT
PRODUCER
Scotia Woodworking
Worcester, MA

The sophisticated use of lighting and highly finished materials blend with the complex geometric forms to appeal to the high end banking market.

31

EXHIBITOR
Purdy Brush
DESIGNER
Kevin West
PRODUCER
Promotion Products Inc.
Portland, OR

An interesting three-dimensional structure calls attention to this $20 \times 20'$ island exhibit.

EXHIBITOR
Sixth Man
DESIGNER
Cathleen M. Durbin
PRODUCER
United Longchamp International
Anaheim, CA

The display cases in this exhibit were made of Meroform elements. They surround a parquet floor with markings like those of a basketball court.

EXHIBITOR
Chiquita Brands
DESIGNER
Gaggan/Griffin
Display Center Showroom
PRODUCER
Nomadic Display
Springfield, VA

This versatile unit was designed for small trade shows and regional meetings. It travels with four sets of roll-out murals and other graphics, to meet the specific marketing situation.

EXHIBITOR
Wolverine Technologies
DESIGNER
Bill Kessler
PRODUCER
Exhibit Builders Inc.
Cleveland, OH

Very dramatic geometric shapes, combined with a sophisticated, truss-based lighting system, resulted in an extremely inviting atmosphere.

EXHIBITOR
Storeel
DESIGNER
Babbe Lee
PRODUCER
United Longchamp International
Atlanta, GA

Samples of the product are essentially the walls and furniture of this exhibit, so visitors can see for themselves how they work. The white Meroform spaceframe ceiling was added for visibility.

EXHIBITOR
Alfa Laval/Thermal
DESIGNER
Michael Edwards
PRODUCER
Exhibitgroup Atlanta
Atlanta, GA

This traveling product display is designed to introduce engineers to the exhibitor's products. Full-size product, cutaways, models, photos and AV presentations were all used to tell the story.

EXHIBITOR
Impel Marketing
DESIGNER
Arthur L. Friedman, Amy Gifford, Claire Noyes
PRODUCER
General Exhibits Inc.
Philadelphia, PA

The black-and-white color of this exhibit attracted attention because of its contrast with the surrounding multi-color exhibits. A large and high video wall drew attention. Samples of the sports cards produced by the exhibitor were displayed on acrylic stands as if each were a jewel. A center conference room provided a confidential area for sales closings.

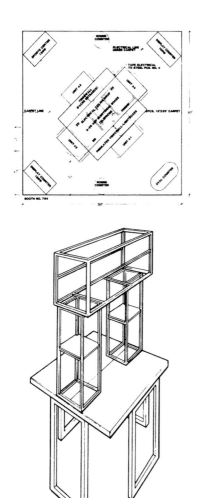

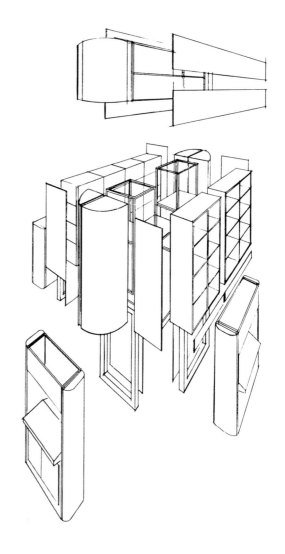

Get Wild. Naturally.

CLEARLY CANADIAN
Sparkling Mineral Water

EXHIBITOR
Clearly Canadian
DESIGNER
Slicko Studios
Vancouver, BC
PRODUCER
Skyline Displays Inc.
Burnsville, MN

The bright colors of the Skyline background bring this photomural to life.

EXHIBITOR
Panasonic Consumer Electronics Group
DESIGNER
John McKeon
PRODUCER
Beitel Displays & Exhibits Inc.
Lawrenceville, NJ

Asked to "romance the product," the designer chose an interesting lighting effect at all product areas in this modular 20 × 40′ island.

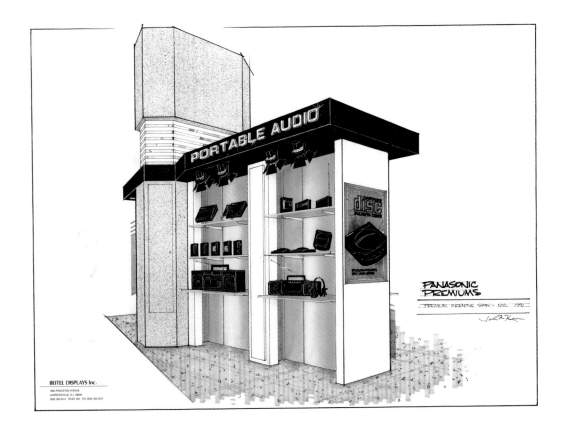

EXHIBITOR
Reliance Electric, Industrial Controls Division
DESIGNER
David Gillespie
PRODUCER
Boss Display Corp.
Columbus, OH

This 20 × 30′ island exhibit is a showcase for Reliance's broad product line and application expertise. Smoked acrylic showcases display active products via simulators and control panels. A free-standing cabinet houses a fully interactive videodisc presentation.

EXHIBITOR
Sunquest Information Systems
DESIGNER
David Gillespie
PRODUCER
Boss Display Corp.
Columbus, OH

This modular exhibit can be set up as a 10′ inline, up to a 30 × 30′ island. It is completely prewired to run an invisible network of data and power lines that connect all the computers in the booth. The Adobe theme is carried throughout, with the Sunquest logo tiled along the tops of the panels, as well as on the ends of the towers.

EXHIBITOR
Peer-Logic
DESIGNER/PRODUCER
Color & Design Exhibits
Portland, OR

With very little time, a low budget, and a company under transition, Peer-Logic told its story by using a stack of its shipping crate, draped in painters canvas to give the notion that the exhibitor was in a transitional phase.

EXHIBITOR
Smith & Nephew United Inc.
DESIGNER
Dave Jeffries, Jr.
PRODUCER
Communication Exhibits Inc.
Canal Fulton, OH

Polarmotion light boxes attract attention on the sides of the 18' center tower. If height restrictions eliminate the tower, the boxes can be used as free standing corner modules.

EXHIBITOR
Columbia Manufacturing Corp.
DESIGNER
Brian Walters
PRODUCER
Communication Exhibits Inc.
Canal Fulton, OH

The soft curves of the towers and the bases contrast with the rigidly rectangular shapes of the product. Placing the company name and logo up high assure their visibility.

EXHIBITOR
Scientific Atlanta
DESIGNER
John Edmonds
PRODUCER
Design South
Atlanta, GA

Designed to demonstrate the technology of HDTV, the exhibit included five demo areas, distinguished by bright colors. Extensive use of perforated metal and clear plexi graphic panels helped to keep the area open and uncluttered.

EXHIBITOR
Johnson Controls
DESIGNER
Anthony M. Stencel
PRODUCER
Derse Exhibits
Milwaukee, WI

A neoclassical architectural style was adopted to introduce a new controls system. The open feeling of the booth encouraged visitors to step into the booth area.

EXHIBITOR
Colgate-Palmolive Co.
DESIGNER
W. Clement Smith
PRODUCER
Dimensional Studios Inc.
Runnemede, NJ

Product becomes the focal point in this simple design which can be used in 10′ increments. Light boxes, lighting fixtures, and shelves for product can be placed anywhere on the back wall.

EXHIBITOR
Eagle Picher Automotive Group
DESIGNER
John Kolin
PRODUCER
Exhibit Builders Inc.
Cleveland, OH

Modules, each representing a different division, clustered around a central tower. A 300-gallon aquarium proved to be a great attention getter.

47

EXHIBITOR
Everbrite Inc.
DESIGNER
Bill Warfel, R. Baird II
PRODUCER
Bill Warfel & Assoc.
Big Bend, WI

Modules served to show examples of the exhibitor's products, using photos, display cases, and actual products. The backgrounds were dark, so as not to distract from the product, with laser-cut logos and bright neon giving the space unity and a jewel-like appearance.

EXHIBITOR
Pro Set
DESIGNER
Linden Bransom
PRODUCER
Exhibit Bilders Inc.
Dallas, TX

White trusses tied together the separate units of this display that featured lines of sporting cards. Emphasis on one card or sport was changed easily to match the "star" who was on hand to autograph trading cards for visitors. The center unit set off a small conference room.

EXHIBITOR
Jerzees Russell
DESIGNER
Mark S. Burns
PRODUCER
Exhibitgroup Atlanta
Atlanta, GA

Known for its outstanding range of color in its garments, the exhibitor wanted to emphasize its reputation as a trendsetter. The display exposed all the colors of their line in four interior wall sections, each with 16 open cubes holding folded garments. Blow-ups of advertising photography add to the excitement.

EXHIBITOR
Advanced Elastomer Systems
DESIGNER
The Robert Falk Group
St. Louis, MO
PRODUCER
Advertiser's Display

The back of this 25 × 50′ exhibit features a long slatwall highlighting the use of rubber replacement parts, whether they are blow molded, injection molded, or extruded. A flag near each sample indicated its national origin. An overhead of flags from around the world added color and supported the international nature of the exhibitor. A triangular conference room was at one end of the space.

EXHIBITOR
Stouffer Hotels & Resorts
DESIGNER
Tom Yurkin, Ken Chang
PRODUCER
Freeman Exhibit Co.
Dallas, TX

Mahogany wood panels, accented by marbleized columns and impressionistic paintings of some of the exhibitor's hotel properties, produce a private club atmosphere.

EXHIBITOR
Pagoda Trading Co./Jeep
DESIGNER
Tom Yurkin
PRODUCER
Freeman Exhibit Co.
Dallas, TX

The product is shoes, but the name is Jeep, and that's enough reason to have a real Jeep in the exhibit. Burled wood, plastic laminates, and leather enhance the products.

EXHIBITOR
Norand Data Systems
DESIGNER
David Eurton, Sr.
PRODUCER
Giltspur/Chicago
Chicago, IL

The corporate product theme of portability and mobility is incorporated into the architecture and graphics of this exhibit. Note the custom workstations with swiveling monitor stands, built-in cable management, and display troughs for 30 and 60 degree viewing angles.

EXHIBITOR
Masterlock Co.
DESIGNER
G.P. Lyons
PRODUCER
Hartwig Exhibitions
Milwaukee, WI

This open design permits the display of a large number of actual products, with a set of different colored banners identifying product groups. A private conference area is on the second level.

EXHIBITOR
John Barrett
DESIGNER
Giltspur/Boston
Boston, MA
PRODUCER
Mead Johnson Pharmaceuticals
Bristol-Myers Squibb Co.

The center of this exhibit was used for a meeting area and as a performance area for a mime depicting anxiety symptoms.

EXHIBITOR
Stouffer Hotels & Resorts
DESIGNER
Tom Yurkin, Ken Chang
PRODUCER
Freeman Exhibit Co.
Dallas, TX

Mahogany wood panels, accented by marbleized columns and impressionistic paintings of some of the exhibitor's hotel properties, produce a private club atmosphere.

EXHIBITOR
Pagoda Trading Co./Jeep
DESIGNER
Tom Yurkin
PRODUCER
Freeman Exhibit Co.
Dallas, TX

The product is shoes, but the name is Jeep, and that's enough reason to have a real Jeep in the exhibit. Burled wood, plastic laminates, and leather enhance the products.

EXHIBITOR
Advanced Elastomer Systems
DESIGNER
The Robert Falk Group
St. Louis, MO
PRODUCER
Advertiser's Display

The back of this 25 × 50′ exhibit features a long slatwall highlighting the use of rubber replacement parts, whether they are blow molded, injection molded, or extruded. A flag near each sample indicated its national origin. An overhead of flags from around the world added color and supported the international nature of the exhibitor. A triangular conference room was at one end of the space.

EXHIBITOR
Zubaz
DESIGNER
Dick Giffin
PRODUCER
Haas Exhibit Marketing
Minneapolis, MN

These photos show two of the configurations which have been used
with these versatile modular units.

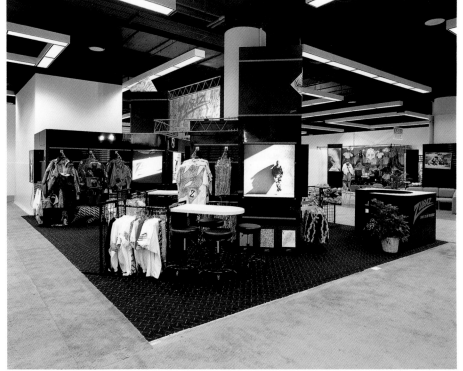

EXHIBITOR
Singer Sewing Co.
DESIGNER
G.P. Lyons
PRODUCER
Hartwig Exhibitions
Milwaukee, WI

This open plan has ample room for product display and demos, with a quiet conference area set off by sliding doors of smoke grey plexi. The overhead structure provides high profile identification and booth illumination.

EXHIBITOR
Badger Meter
DESIGNER
P. Graw, G.P. Lyons
PRODUCER
Hartwig Exhibitions
Milwaukee, WI

The overhead structure is of custom fabric components, from Moss. Product is displayed on custom racks, and kiosks hold illustrations, a monitor, and literature storage.

EXHIBITOR
Rhone-Poulenc
DESIGNER
Stephen Walsh
PRODUCER
John Oldham Studios Inc.
Wethersfield, CT

This 1,500 square foot exhibit includes a private conference room, four open conference area/workstations, and an 18′ long food island where samples were served. The exhibit was open and dramatic, while bold graphics supported the exhibitor's varied food industries.

EXHIBITOR
Centocor Inc.
DESIGNER/PRODUCER
Kitzing Inc.
Chicago, IL

A world leader in monoclone antibodies, Centocor required a strong brand presence, on-aisle sell stations, and an exhibit capable of being down-sized to a 20 × 20′ island.

EXHIBITOR
Copeland Corporation
DESIGNER/PRODUCER
L.W. Milby Inc. Exhibits
New Carlisle, OH

The long, curved, undulating back wall includes 2 fiber-optic maps and 3-D light boxes. There are four free-standing video units with product display areas on either side. The monitor in the center describes the uses of the products on display.

EXHIBITOR
WilTel
DESIGNER
Robert Meyer, William Wilson
PRODUCER
Pingel Displays Inc.
St. Louis, MO

A compatible mix of custom decor and Nimlok components provides a clean, contemporary environment, highlighting a video wall.

EXHIBITOR
Caere Corporation
DESIGNER
Mitchell Mauk, Mauk Design
San Francisco, CA
PRODUCER
Bluepeter
San Francisco, CA

This exhibit dimensionally demonstrates the way in which optical character recognition software works, using oversized symbolic components and bright red arrows carrying copy.

EXHIBITOR
Chubb Group of Insurance Companies
DESIGNER
Dave McMillan MCM
Somerville, NJ
PRODUCER
Mount Vernon Displays Inc.
Prospect Park, NJ

This exhibit consists of, essentially, three elements. Two—a cylinder and a cube—are slotted, while the third is a panel which slides into a slot for support. Lighting elements are mounted on top of the panel. These units can be placed in any configuration, and panels can be made up for any audience and any marketing objective.

EXHIBITOR
Chase Manhattan Leasing
DESIGNER
David Hurt, Don Hessler
PRODUCER
Pingel Displays Inc.
St. Louis, MO

A massive 16′ high tower suggests corporate strength and a feeling of permanence. The pierce-cut, internally illuminated company name offers high visibility. As a final touch, a reflective blue mirror treatment projects the refined grace of the company.

EXHIBITOR
Pan American Seed
DESIGNER
Serge Eloi
PRODUCER
United Longchamp International
Chicago, IL

Handouts with questions about floriculture encouraged visitors to find the answers in the copy on light box graphics. The very clean, hi-tech structure formed a good background to the warmth of the natural flowers.

EXHIBITOR
Protocol Systems
DESIGNER
Alan Ransenberg
PRODUCER
Promotion Products Inc.
Portland, OR

An unusual use of a thermoclear sheet in tension, and backlit with floods, and carrying the company logo, features this unusual booth that is bound to attract attention.

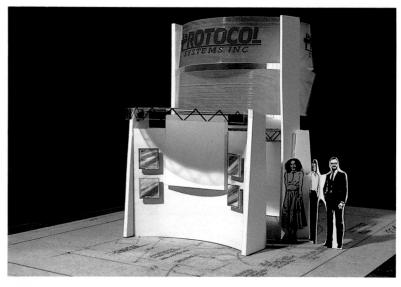

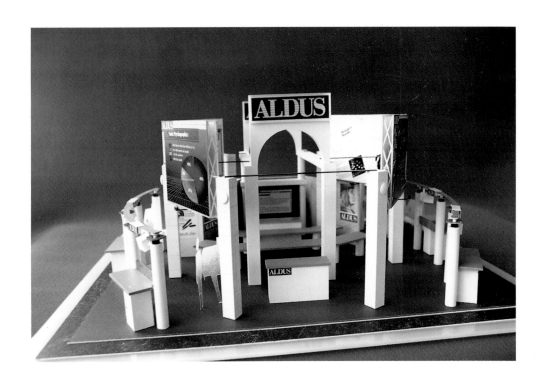

EXHIBITOR
Aldus
DESIGNER
Kevin West
PRODUCER
Promotion Products Inc.
Portland, OR

A central demonstration area was surrounded by individual demo stations on the periphery. The overhead projector screens allowed for constantly changing appearance.

EXHIBITOR
Sherwin-Williams Co.
DESIGNER/PRODUCER
Rogers Display Co.
Mentor, OH

The modular units devised for
this client give a great deal of
flexibility, both as to booth configuration and for a variety of product
and service lines.

EXHIBITOR
Er-We-Pa
DESIGNER
Babbe Lee
PRODUCER
United Longchamp International
Atlanta, GA

Chrome Merotruss elements permit
the exhibitor's name to be raised
up to the maximum height without
undue expense.

CHAPTER 3

EXHIBITS ON THE BIG SIDE

1,601 – 4,000 ft² (149 – 371 m²)

EXHIBITOR
Specialized Bike Components
DESIGNER/PRODUCER
Color & Design Exhibits Inc.
Portland, OR

More than 24 bikes are displayed in this 50 × 60′ booth, along with 8 areas for related products. Each bike stands on a bent aluminum stand, surmounted by a distinctive white canopy. The product areas use slatwall on two sides to display products from water bottles to shoes. The conference rooms utilize a keypoint system for configuration and flexibility, and there is a semi-private theater.

Two identical exhibits, one for the United States and the other for Europe, were constructed at the same time.

EXHIBITOR
Johnson Controls Inc.
DESIGNER
Michael Saubert
PRODUCER
Convention Exhibits Inc.
Chicago, IL

The product—plastic bottles—is displayed in museum type showcases with color corrected lighting. Corporate identification is internally illuminated and visible from all directions. Three conference rooms are contained in the center of the structure.

EXHIBITOR
CBS Fox Video
DESIGNER
Matthew Wycislak, Michael Saubert
PRODUCER
Convention Exhibits Inc.
Chicago, IL

The exhibit included a mini film studio to produce special promotional video tapes for show attendees. It could also transfer video images of booth visitors onto T-shirts.

EXHIBITOR
Cooper Rolls
DESIGNER
Dave Jeffries, Jr., Brian Walters
PRODUCER
Communication Exhibits Inc.
Canal Fulton, OH

Curved towers with stairwells support a second floor hospitality suite and two private conference areas, creating a strong architectural shape which provides controlled lighting to the open sales floor below.

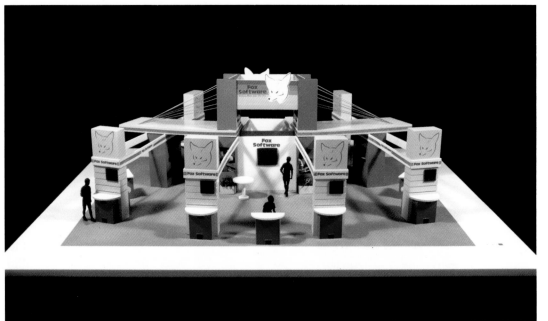

EXHIBITOR
Fox Software
DESIGNER
Lisa Montgomery
PRODUCER
Denby Associates
Princeton, NJ

This 40 × 50′ island booth features the exhibitor's distinctive logo. Demonstration areas fan out from the central tower and conference room structure, with workstations strategically placed along the perimeter of the exhibit.

EXHIBITOR
Instrumentation Lab
DESIGNER
John Edmonds
PRODUCER
Design South
Atlanta, GA

In order to present a variety of products in a unified environment, the designer turned to modular components. The units used custom-made aluminum substructure and facing, as well as wood and plastics. The metal construction provided stability and allowed for the cantilever design, difficult to accomplish with wood.

EXHIBITOR
Rohm & Haas
DESIGNER
Mitchell Gilbert
PRODUCER
Dimensional Studios Inc.
Runnemede, NJ

About 90 percent of the materials used in this display are products of the exhibitor.

EXHIBITOR
SuperMac
DESIGNER
David Liau
PRODUCER
Exhibitgroup San Francisco
South San Francisco, CA

The corrugated composite red tubing contrasted with the truss-style open framing to call attention to this booth. The tubing also served to hold the electrical connections for the computers and the lighting. The towers are adjustable, and the exhibit can be set up into 20 × 40′ and 20 × 20′ spaces, as well as the 40 × 50′ configuration shown here.

EXHIBITOR
B.F. Goodrich
DESIGNER
John Kolin
PRODUCER
Exhibit Builders Inc.
Cleveland, OH

Excitement was achieved with very dramatic colors, bold graphics and product displays, neon-accented lighting, and a live demonstration. Actual plastic prototypes were generated at the booth, using computer-laser equipment.

EXHIBITOR
Brach's
DESIGNER
Jeffrey Burke
PRODUCER
Exhibit by Design Inc.
Arlington Heights, IL

This exhibit is both fun and elegant. The colored awnings, with their pink and purple stripes, derive from the company's first building. Here they were supported by double-sided product modules, and lit from beneath with halogen strip lighting, so they were visible and recognizable from across the floor.

The structure at the end of the canopies held two private conference rooms, each with a full ceiling, and a storeroom. The walls of the conference rooms that faced the back aisles were of $2 \times 2'$ textured plexi.

EXHIBITOR
ITT Hartford
DESIGNER
Mark Holme
PRODUCER
Giltspur/Boston
Avon, MA

This exhibit, designed for the annual meeting of the American Association of Retired Persons, is intended to give older consumers information on the comfort and safety features of various automobiles. The exhibit includes a theater seating 50 and three interactive video demos to simulate braking.

EXHIBITOR
Carl Zeiss Inc.
DESIGNER
Tim Prinzing
PRODUCER
Giltspur/Rochester
Rochester, NY

The truss towers, stabilized with threaded rods and turnbuckles, made an interesting visual statement. They supported double-sided light boxes, $60 \times 60''$, as well as the circular background and header. Color monitors in the demo areas were mounted in boxes between truss sections, and could be swiveled to allow the entire cabinet to be repositioned freely.

EXHIBITOR
TRW
DESIGNER/PRODUCER
Giltspur/Pittsburgh
Pittsburgh, PA

This demonstration of air-bag operation was light-activated, and related to five color-coded modalities on the wire car. The graphics were done in German and Japanese, in addition to English, for use in those countries.

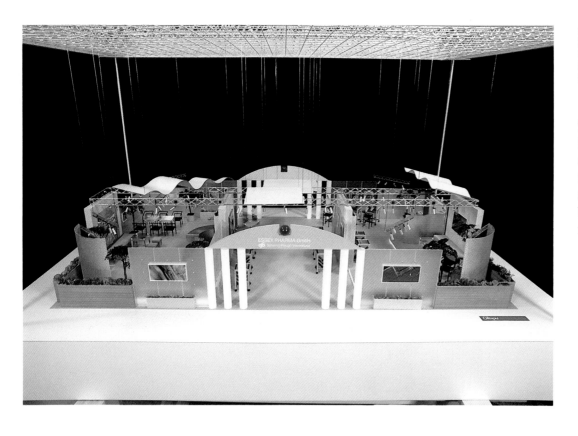

EXHIBITOR
Schering/Plough
DESIGNER/PRODUCER
Giltspur/Pittsburgh
Pittsburgh, PA

This exhibit included a number of interactive computer terminals, scattered throughout the multi-tiered floor. Parts of the exhibit, shown in Berlin, Germany, were built on-site, following a European rather than American approach.

EXHIBITOR
Formica Corporation
DESIGNER
Kenneth R. Konke
PRODUCER
Heritage Display Group
Dallas, TX

The surface of the entire exhibit is covered with the exhibitor's products. The structure is very modular and can be reconfigured into a wide variety of sizes.

EXHIBITOR
Hon Company
DESIGNER/PRODUCER
Kitzing Inc.
Chicago, IL

The exhibit is organized by functional product areas, with the new fully-articulated chair given the central spot. Back-lit dimensional logos gave the exhibitor strong company identification from all angles.

EXHIBITOR
American Association of Retired Persons
DESIGNER
Babbe Lee
PRODUCER
United Longchamp International
Atlanta, GA

The American Association of Retired Persons wanted to provide an attractive, distinctive lounge area at its own convention. The front information counter served exhibitors and attendees alike. Behind it was an area with comfortable seating. The arches defined the spaces, simply and economically.

EXHIBITOR
Sun Microsystems
DESIGNER
Mitchell Mauk, Francis Parker
Mauk Design, San Francisco, CA
PRODUCER
FM Productions
Brisbane, CA

Vivid colors and unusual graphic treatment, in an enclosed environment, made this stand out from its neighbors. Special lighting, especially around the entrances, drew attendees into the space.

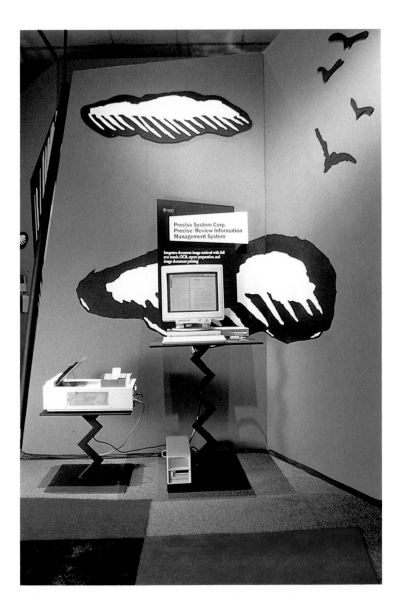

CONTINUED

EXHIBITOR
McDonald's Corp./Real Estate Division
DESIGNER
W. E. Murphy & Co.
Chicago, IL
PRODUCER
Nomadic Display
Springfield, VA

This exhibit, using Space Strut, is a breeze to install. It takes only half an hour because the elements unfold and set up manually without tools.

THE GIANTS ON THE FLOOR

>4,000 ft² (>371 m²)

EXHIBITOR
Unionbay Sportswear
DESIGNER/PRODUCER
Color & Design Exhibits Inc.
Portland, OR

In order to help the visitor concentrate on the Unionbay line of clothing, the exhibit was designed to be set off from the busy show floor. The entire space, 40 × 110′, was raised by a floor, and the design had openings on the sides and ends only, to create a very separate atmosphere.

Within the booth, there were four different selling areas, each set up for easy, organized access. Tempered glass panels in front, combined with a rough board, gave the exhibit an earthly yet sophisticated feel.

EXHIBITOR
IBM
DESIGNER
Joel Katzowitz
PRODUCER
Design South
Atlanta, GA

With four key messages to deliver to the attendees, a separate area, or environment, was devoted to each message. Six one-on-one demonstrations supported each environment, a reduction from 110 demos the previous year.

With four focus areas, the exhibit could be more open and less intimidating than in previous years. The counters were supported by aluminum columns which gave the illusion of floating members. An aluminum superstructure permitted great distances to be spanned with small open structures. This contributed to the feeling of openness, and incidentally, reduced show service costs by about 50 percent.

EXHIBITOR
Dow Chemical Co.
DESIGNER
J. Patrick Mason
PRODUCER
Design Craftsmen Inc.
Midland, MI

Tensioned fabric was used to achieve visual impact and adaptability, and to reduce fabrication costs and shipping weight. The cylinders were lit from the interior to give the entire space an intriguing glow.

When visitors entered the "Success in Motion" enclosure, they found themselves on a turntable, 35′ in diameter, viewing a continuous, multi-media presentation.

The space also contained two upper-level conference rooms.

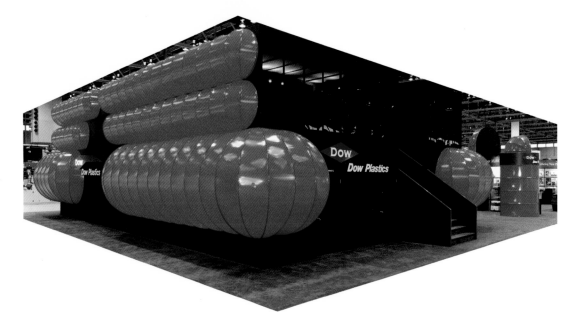

EXHIBITOR
Xerox
DESIGNER
David Uzarowski
PRODUCER
Giltspur/Rochester
Rochester, NY

This exhibit is distinguished for a number of demonstration areas, which provided comfortable seating for large numbers of visitors. Elevated workstations and video walls were used to tell the product story.

EXHIBITOR
Subaru of America
DESIGNER
Will Freemire
PRODUCER
Giltspur/Pittsburgh
Pittsburgh, PA

The cars are the thing at a public auto show, and here they are set off by structures with an anodized, stamped aluminum skin, highlighted by blue rear-illuminated letters. The traction center, with a car on top, serves as an eye-catcher and houses a demonstration theater.

CONTINUED

EXHIBITOR
Reebok International Inc.
DESIGNER
Cassandra Henning
PRODUCER
C. Henning Studios
Atlanta, GA

The exterior of this exhibit was made up of oversize shoe boxes, whose walls, visible from the aisles, presented new commercials about the products in the box. An entrance at one end led to an enclosed mall, at the other end of which was a demonstration stage backed by a 25-screen video wall. Along both sides were individual "shops," each devoted to one product segment. These shops were designed so that they could be used individually and in combinations for smaller shows.

CONTINUED

EXHIBITOR
Coca-Cola Company
DESIGNER
Cassandra Henning
PRODUCER
C. Henning Studios
Atlanta, GA

Some of the design elements in this exhibit, like the bottle-like supports for the upper level and the spectacular sprays of lights from the over-size bottles, were inspired by the Coca-Cola museum in Atlanta.

EXHIBITOR
Reebok International Ltd.
DESIGNER
Cassandra Henning
PRODUCER
C. Henning Studios
Atlanta, GA

The theme for this exhibit was "Back to School," and visitors were treated to a scaled-down high school. It had a realistic facade, classrooms, gymnasium and sports stadium. One of the features was a real school bus, one side of which had been removed so that the interior could be used as the setting for a fashion show.

CONTINUED

EXHIBITOR
NovoNordisk
DESIGNER
Neils Wibroe
Denmark
PRODUCER
Nomadic Display
Springfield, VA

This spectacular use of SpaceStrut frame for the ceiling of this open display unified the space and provided an easy lighting solution.

EXHIBITOR
Masco Corporation
DESIGNER/PRODUCER
Kitzing Inc.
Chicago, IL

All the Masco companies were represented in this 29,000 square foot exhibit, the largest in the history of the National Association of Home Builders show. There was a unified corporate tower and beam assembly. Special attraction areas like the home plans gallery built visitor traffic throughout the area.

EXHIBITOR
Toshiba America Information Systems Inc.
DESIGNER
i e Design
Tustin, CA
PRODUCER
Exhibitree Inc.
San Francisco, CA

To introduce its new color laptop computer, Toshiba built its exhibit around a massive central structure, 50′ long, 16′ high, 10′ deep, on which were placed 7′ high letters. This unit was painted white, but illuminated from below by lights arranged along its base. Each light had 16 different colored gels, which were controlled by a central computer, so there was a constantly changing color pattern. The central structure held conference rooms at both ends, while the central portion contained storage and electrical controls.

EXHIBITOR
Husky Injection Molding Systems
DESIGNER/PRODUCER
Kitzing Inc.
Chicago, IL

This large exhibit, sponsored by a leading manufacturer of injection molding equipment and its two sales partners, showed new technologies and systems in a showroom setting. It combined custom components and leased units.

EXHIBITOR
Square D Company
DESIGNER
McMillan Group
Wilton, CT
PRODUCER
Heritage Display Group
St. Paul, MN

This large exhibit, which spans a
show aisle, is impressive because
of its technical/heavy industry
look, and for its extreme modularity of custom exhibit parts.

CONTINUED

EXHIBITOR
Digital Equipment Corporation
DESIGNER
Babbe Lee
PRODUCER
United Longchamp International
Atlanta, GA

The demonstration stage, at one end of the exhibit, could be used for live performances as well as a video presentation. Behind the stage were many demonstration areas, marked off with vertical banners which called attention to specific product groupings.

EXHIBITOR
Sony Corporation
DESIGNER
Blumlein Assoc.
PRODUCER
Structural Display Inc.
Long Island City, NY

The standard exhibit hall space was given distinction with a ceiling of canvas, indirect lighting, special display areas, and a theater with surround sound.

CHAPTER 5

MULTI-LEVEL STRUCTURES

EXHIBITOR
Panasonic Office Automation Group
DESIGNER
John McKeon
PRODUCER
Beitel Displays & Exhibits Inc.
Lawrenceville, NJ

The second level of this 70 × 110′ exhibit features ten private meeting rooms. Each group of related products had its own set of demo stations, some of them in satellite construction. There was also very impressive corporate identification.

EXHIBITOR
GE Medical Systems
DESIGNER
GE Medical Systems Exhibit Staff and
Suppliers
PRODUCER
Expotechnik Systems; Derse Exhibits
Milwaukee, WI

Two massive double-deck units,
each with its own stairway, are
connected by a bridge. On the
second level are check rooms, sec-
retarial pool, monitored message
centers, a learning center, lounge,
and three conference rooms.

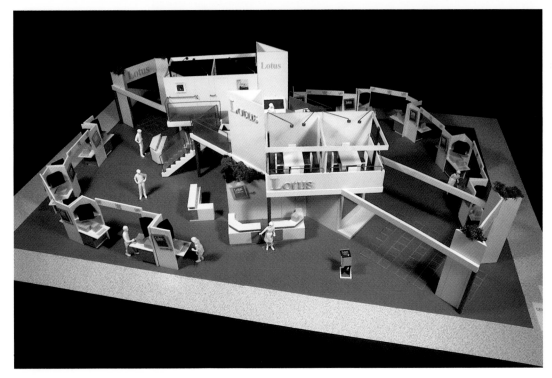

EXHIBITOR
Lotus
DESIGNER
Lisa Montgomery
PRODUCER
Denby Associates
Princeton, NJ

This 50 × 80′ two-story island can also work in a number of different configurations, down to a 10 × 20′ inline. The upper story has four private conference rooms, two open seating areas, and two 30′ towers that carry the corporate logo. On the main floor are 17 product demo stations, as well as two presentation areas and four enclosed rooms. The colors used throughout are greys and whites, with a variety of textured metals used in their natural silver color. The metal elements accent workstations, desks, stairs, and railings.

EXHIBITOR
Mitsubishi Electronics
DESIGNER
Charles W. Willoughby
PRODUCER
Exhibit Technology Inc.
Worcester, MA

A two-story office is reached by a stairway whose well encloses the electrical controls. All connections are concealed in 16' long canopies which reach out to ten octagonal demonstration stations.

The exhibit elements can handle various installations ranging from $20 \times 20'$ to $50 \times 80'$.

EXHIBITOR
Rockwell Graphic Systems
DESIGNER
Anthony M. Stencel
PRODUCER
Derse Exhibits
Milwaukee, WI

Three spectacular towers dominate this large exhibit. Each 30′ high tower uses polylite and aluminum. Flexible neon tubing is wrapped around the 85′ circumference of the towers.

EXHIBITOR
Linotype AG
DESIGNER
Ludwig Ense
PRODUCER
Ernst F. Ambrosius & Sohn; Fairconsult
Köln, Germany

Small conference rooms ran along a corridor on the upper level, which was reached by a wide staircase which led to an open area in which a number of small group meetings could be held. The ceiling, based on an abstract concept of a computer electronic element, was a conspicuous object as one mounted the stairs. The ground floor was divided into product demo areas, demarcated by horizontal color bars which matched the colored light fixtures atop the massive columns.

EXHIBITOR
Felix Böttcher GmbH & Co.
DESIGNER
Ludwig Ense
PRODUCER
Born & Strukamp/Fairconsult
Köln, Germany

Note the yellow columns which support the second floor. These are based on the exhibitor's product—printing rolls—while the undulating shape of the deck suggests rolls of printing paper. The upper level had a refreshment counter and many small tables with an excellent view of the show floor.

EXHIBITOR
Murata Business Systems
DESIGNER
Randy Bennett
PRODUCER
Heritage Display Group
Dallas, TX

The unusual shape of this two-story exhibit made it stand out on the show floor. Placing the product displays at the bases of the upper deck supports gave an open feeling to the display and permitted an easy flow-through of traffic.

EXHIBITOR
Picker International
DESIGNER/PRODUCER
Rogers Display Co.
Mentor, OH

The massive structure that housed the second level area gave this exhibit a dominating position and great recognition at the busy Radiological Society of North America show.

EXHIBITOR
Motoman
DESIGNER/PRODUCER
L.W. Milby Inc. Exhibits
New Carlisle, OH

The upper level, reached by spiral staircases, has two semi-private meeting areas. From it one can overlook a center courtyard which features various moving robotic equipment. There are two private conference areas on the ground level. The 12′ high, angular, backlit corner identification units clearly mark off the display area.

EXHIBITOR
Keebler Company
DESIGNER/PRODUCER
Stevens Exhibits/Displays Inc.
Chicago, IL

The spacious upper-level conference area is supported by lightweight fiberglass I-beams. The stage area has a changeable background.

EXHIBITOR
Philips Medical Systems North America
DESIGNER
Stephen Walsh
PRODUCER
John Oldham Studios Inc.
Wethersfield, CT

The central two-story structure not only contains space for conference rooms, but it also provides support for large, hanging medical equipment. The exhibit maintains an open appearance while showing more than 60 actual working systems and multiple demo areas.

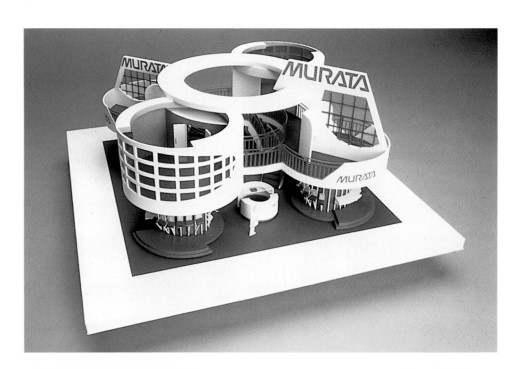

EXHIBITOR
Murata Business Systems
DESIGNER
Randy Bennett
PRODUCER
Heritage Display Group
Dallas, TX

The unusual shape of this two-story exhibit made it stand out on the show floor. Placing the product displays at the bases of the upper deck supports gave an open feeling to the display and permitted an easy flow-through of traffic.

EXHIBITOR
Felix Böttcher GmbH & Co.
DESIGNER
Ludwig Ense
PRODUCER
Born & Strukamp/Fairconsult
Köln, Germany

Note the yellow columns which support the second floor. These are based on the exhibitor's product—printing rolls—while the undulating shape of the deck suggests rolls of printing paper. The upper level had a refreshment counter and many small tables with an excellent view of the show floor.

EXHIBITOR
Rubbermaid Inc.
DESIGNER
Robert Linden
PRODUCER
Rogers Display Co.
Mentor, OH

With a large line of varied items to show, the lower level uses walls and shelves for product, while the upper level is devoted largely to space for sales conferences. Illuminated signs with the company name are elevated to catch the eye from all parts of the show.

EXHIBITOR
Russell Athletic
DESIGNER
Babbe Lee
PRODUCER
United Longchamp International
Atlanta, GA

Designed for the very competitive Super Show, which has limited space, this exhibit gives Russell extra office space above the essential sales and demonstration areas. The elevated structure also provided extra visibility. The Octanorm Double Deck system was used.

EXHIBITOR
Ellesse
DESIGNER
Cassandra Henning
PRODUCER
C. Henning Studios
Atlanta, GA

A spiral staircase led up to a cat-walk which joined the two sections of the multilevel booth. The lower level housed the display show-rooms, and the upper level workstations. The rear of the booth was set up for a presentation stage and a courtyard-like hospi-tality area.

EXHIBITOR
Coca-Cola Company
DESIGNER
Cassandra Henning
PRODUCER
C. Henning Studios
Atlanta, GA

Spiral staircases that led to the upper level lounge area were concealed inside two 14′ replicas of cans that flanked the 20 screen video wall. The lower level contained conference, stage and technical areas. Giant product logos and monitor towers on the sides of the booth provided additional interest.

CHAPTER

EXHIBITS WITH DEMOS AND PRESENTATIONS

EXHIBITOR
Cincinnati Children's Museum
DESIGNER
Charles P. Koch
PRODUCER
Ad-Ex International,
Cincinnati, OH

This straightforward exhibit, installed in a show called "All About Kids," drew children into participating in the interactive displays, and demonstrated to adults what the museum was all about.

EXHIBITOR
Harry Diamond Labs
DESIGNER
Wayne Nicolette
PRODUCER
Adler Display Inc.
Baltimore, MD

This demo unit is a scale model of an enemy target, depicting a supply depot, an assembly area, and an air target. A push button starts an audio explanation of the difference between a proximity and an impact fused missile. The audio is synchronized with a fiber optics display behind a two-way mirror demonstration.

EXHIBITOR
Goal Systems International
DESIGNER
David Gillespie
PRODUCER
Boss Display Corp.
Columbus, OH

The modular units can be set up in a variety of configurations. The pre-assembled kiosks roll into place, get plugged in, and they are ready to serve as demo stations. All graphics are back-lit and interchangeable. The 4' header extensions can be set on top of the kiosks or on the floor as signage.

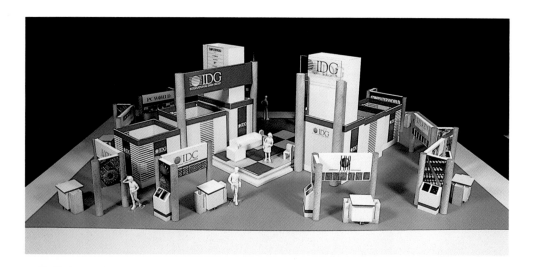

EXHIBITOR
IDG Communications
DESIGNER
Lisa Montgomery
PRODUCER
Denby Associates
Princeton, NJ

Multi-functional components permit this exhibit to grow from $10 \times 20'$ inlines to a $50 \times 70'$ island. Each of the exhibitor's ten computer industry magazines has its own work area which contains two large light boxes, a sales counter, and magazine distribution bins. Four private conference rooms surround a central open conference area.

EXHIBITOR
Cross Creek Apparel
DESIGNER
Echelon Design Inc.
PRODUCER
Exhibit Builders Inc.
Cleveland, OH

This island exhibit resembles a southern home, in keeping with the exhibitor's line of traditional apparel. Five presentation areas are available for small group viewing of specific pieces, and a sixth area can be used for more informal discussions. Natural red oak is used to reinforce the country style.

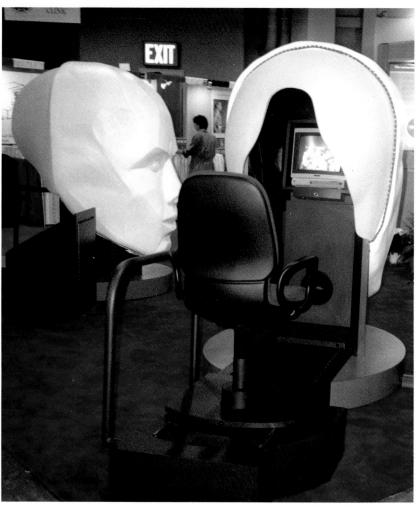

EXHIBITOR
Glaxo Inc.
DESIGNER
Paul Murphy, Bruce Nickerson
PRODUCER
Giltspur/Boston
Avon, MA

This unit is actually a simulator that puts the visitor into a migraine headache environment. It combines video, computer-generated images, and lighting to achieve its effects.

EXHIBITOR
Eastman Kodak Co.
DESIGNER
Kirk Goltry
PRODUCER
Giltspur/Rochester
Rochester, NY

Each side of the four towers holds a workstation demo area, encouraging good visibility and traffic flow. This replaced an earlier version which seemed to wall in the exhibit.

EXHIBITOR
U.S. Sprint
DESIGNER
Mark S. Burns
PRODUCER
Exhibitgroup Atlanta
Atlanta, GA

A special demonstration area permitted the exhibitor to explain its teleconferencing capabilities by involving booth visitors in an actual conference. A nine-monitor presentation told the story, using TV cameras directed at the audience to bring them into the action.

EXHIBITOR
3M
DESIGNER/PRODUCER
CES
St. Paul, MN

3M Micrographics considers itself the bridging technology of the future for document storage and retrieval. The concept was demonstrated in a comfortable central theater, using a live presentation. The red bridges reminded visitors of the theme, and tied the units together. Individual demo workstations were easily reached from the aisles.

EXHIBITOR
Keithley Instruments Inc.
DESIGNER
Keith Gamble
PRODUCER
Promotional Fixtures Inc.
Rittman, OH

This exhibit, whose sections face across an aisle, is made of totally assembled 5′ modules which simply roll out of their crates, keeping installation and dismantling to a minimum. Their modular design permits total flexibility in arrangement. The counters are removable to accommodate any product mix. All graphic panels and light boxes are interchangeable.

EXHIBITOR
Tri-Con Industries Inc.
DESIGNER
Noreen Dyczkowski
PRODUCER
Design Fabrication

This exhibit was designed to be used to build the image of the company. It is open and roomy for demonstrating new products. It is shown here as a 20 × 20′ island.

EXHIBITOR
Sharp Electronics
DESIGNER
Ray Crouch
PRODUCER
Giltspur/Rochester
Rochester, NY

Private conference rooms were reached by a balcony that overlooked the interior of this large exhibit. Interest was added by life-size castings of people, some of them using Sharp products. The space also held a theater for product presentations.

EXHIBITOR
Nintendo of America
DESIGNER
Kevin West
PRODUCER
Promotion Products Inc.
Portland, OR

Visitors were invited to play games on special front projection screens, while seated in special game seats with stereo sound, in addition to the standard monitor games. There was also a small video stage.

EXHIBITOR
Marlow Surgical Technologies, Gynescope
DESIGNER
Herbert N. Byers, Jr.
PRODUCER
Rogers Display Co.
Mentor, OH

This exhibit features an interactive surgical demonstration stand, with the ability to show aspiration and irrigation products. The design is within the context of typical medical surroundings, using a white plastic ABS finish, and clean, rounded corners.

EXHIBITOR
Philip Morris USA
DESIGNER
Jonathan Arkin Design
PRODUCER
Structural Display Inc.
Long Island City, NY

The highlight of this exhibit is an interactive computer that offers profitability information. A laser gun game creates a competitive spirit. The custom design offers great modularity. By removing plexi graphic panels, it can then accept video walls, showcases, and so on.

CHAPTER 7
OTHER THAN TRADE SHOWS

EXHIBITOR
Baltimore Gas & Electric
DESIGNER
J. Gardiner Meade; Judy Blumberg
PRODUCER
Accent Exhibits Designs & Displays
Baltimore, MD

This lobby display shows the history of the Spring Gardens plant. It includes the story of the use of natural gas, and then how to manufacture it. The display incorporates actual sepia tones from the first part of the century, architectural drawings from the late 1800s, patent drawings (old and crumbly), and original lab equipment.

FROM CANDLES TO CALORIES

During its first forty years as an industry, gas was primarily used for light. The quality of gas was measured in candle power. Then, in 1855, Robert Wilhelm von Bunsen developed a gas burner capable of producing an extremely hot, smokeless flame, and thus created entirely new applications for gas as a fuel for heating and cooking. After 1900, electricity became the dominant fuel for lighting, and gas was fast becoming a source of heat alone. Gauging gas by its ability to produce light had become outdated.

New standards of gas quality involved heat value. The metric standard was the calorie: the amount of energy needed to raise one gram of water one degree Celsius. The English standard became the Btu: the energy required to raise a pound of water one degree Fahrenheit. Regardless of the standard employed, however, the instrument used to measure heating value, also developed by Bunsen, was the calorimeter.

Various calorimeters were used at Spring Gardens, yet all performed the same task: each determined how many degrees a measured weight of water was raised by burning a measured volume of gas.

Originally, the Maryland Public Service Commission set a standard of 650 Btu for manufactured gas, which it later reduced to 500. Meeting the legal standard required much testing and mixing.

Sectional Elevation of Hot Side of Benches. Water Gas Plant Spring Garden Station.

Scale 3/16 in. = 1 ft.

CONSOLIDATED GAS CO OF BALTIMORE CITY
1897

EXHIBITOR
Baltimore Gas & Electric
DESIGNER
J. Gardiner Meade
Parker Pennington
PRODUCER
Accent Exhibits Designs & Displays
Baltimore, MD

The history of gas and electricity was outlined in seven large windows, five of them on a main, busy street. People waiting for a bus and mid-day shoppers alike take the time to examine the windows. They are filled with artifacts and photos from each of the periods of the past. What seems to be a continuous neon tube runs through the historical windows and ties the units together.

CONTINUED

EXHIBITOR
Mercy Medical Center
DESIGNER
Gary Ebersole, Elizabeth Lockett
PRODUCER
Adler Display Inc.
Baltimore, MD

Two lobby kiosks are made up of enclosed glass showcases, and a combination of back-lit duratrans, mounted photos, and silkscreened graphics. The display is designed to be prominent without obstructing the traffic flow through a busy elevator lobby.

EXHIBITOR
Mannington Mills
DESIGNER
Melanie Wood, Mannington Mills
Mark Burns, Exhibitgroup
PRODUCER
Exhibitgroup Atlanta
Atlanta, GA

This project required the complete renovation of the existing showroom in the Atlanta Merchandise Mart. The client's product was used as floor covering in each individual product area, as well as in the new product demonstration area. New point-of-purchase units were incorporated into the design to display new product.

EXHIBITOR
NYNEX
DESIGNER
John Sereduke
PRODUCER
Dimensional Studios Inc.
Runnemede, NJ

This product showroom was designed to be adaptable to various locations, and still keep the same tone. Each back-lit panel corresponds with a product which is hooked up and ready to use. Continuous power track allows for diverse placement of light boxes.

EXHIBITOR
Wilsonart
DESIGNER/PRODUCER
TW Design & Construction
Dallas, TX

This unique presentation used steel cables suspended from the overhead structure, anchored by concrete pyramids on a brushed aluminum floor. The use of natural materials, including granite, aluminum, steel, verdigris tin panels, underscored the inherent beauty of the broad spectrum of colors and patterns in the laminate product line.

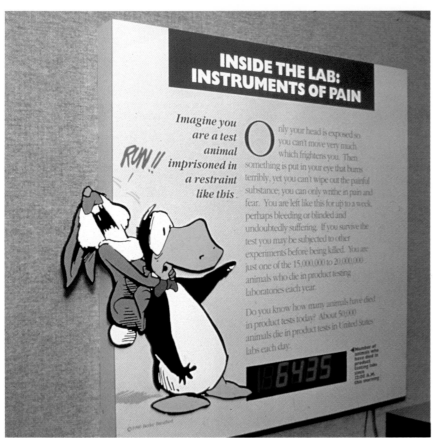

EXHIBITOR
NE Anti-Vivisection Society
DESIGNER
Peggy Kirk, Jane Corbus
PRODUCER
Giltspur/Boston
Avon, MA

This traveling van exhibit is designed to promote cruelty-free testing on animals for consumer products. The artwork was adapted from the Bloom County comic strip, with the permission of the cartoonist, Berke Brethed.

EXHIBITOR
AT&T Network Systems
DESIGNER
Jim Sella
PRODUCER
Giltspur/Chicago
Chicago, IL

This permanent installation, in San Ramon, California, permits the client to make product presentations in a comfortable, controlled environment.

The entry is distinguished by a mosaic of wrapped lead, burnished stainless steel, cut stone, and ceramic tile, which creates a dimensional backdrop for an edge-lit, etched glass main entry graphic.

EXHIBITOR
NYNEX Mobile Communications
DESIGNER
Steven Levy, Graphics 55
PRODUCER
Mount Vernon Displays Inc.
Prospect Park, NJ

There's no question what is being featured in this product showroom when your eye is caught by an 11' model of a modular phone. Other instruments and accessories are neatly displayed in showcases contained in pedestals.

EXHIBITOR
Emergency Networks Inc.
DESIGNER
Michael Peterson
PRODUCER
Heritage Display Group/Dallas
Dallas, TX

The van carries a complete outdoor exhibit, which includes two audio-visual kiosks, a model kiosk, and two contest entry units. The interior of the van is designed to look like an office lobby, using a large black-on-black halo-lit logo, as well as a conference room and a hospitality bar.

EXHIBITOR
Osram
DESIGNER
Ber Verhaar
PRODUCER
Laarhoven Design BV
Zoeterwoude, The Netherlands

This multifunctional room can be used for product presentations, as well as a background for more formal lectures and meetings. Its elements can even be adapted to trade show use.

EXHIBITOR
MCI
DESIGNER
Lorenc Design
PRODUCER
Designers Workshop
Chamblee, GA

This permanent corporate exhibit, 8' high and 64' long, was designed to communicate the motion, energy, and devotion of MCI consumer service personnel.

Ground aluminum panels are flat against the walls at the entrance, but as the triangular space widens, the panels progressively angle out at the bottom, while the tops remain flat against the wall, creating a warped wall. As the bottom edges gradually lift off the floor, lit by track lighting, and with wall, ceiling and carpet all black, the exhibit appears to hover.

A video monitor exhibits current MCI news, events, and activity.

CONTINUED

171

EXHIBITOR
Osram
DESIGNER
Ber Verhaar
PRODUCER
Laarhoven Design BV
Zoeterwoude, The Netherlands

This multifunctional room can be used for product presentations, as well as a background for more formal lectures and meetings. Its elements can even be adapted to trade show use.

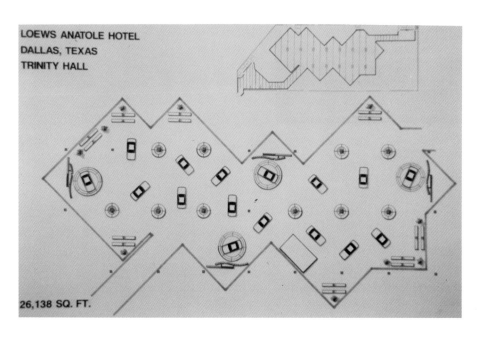

LOEWS ANATOLE HOTEL
DALLAS, TEXAS
TRINITY HALL

26,138 SQ. FT.

EXHIBITOR
Mitsubishi Motor Sales of America
DESIGNER
Paul Hemsworth
PRODUCER
George P. Johnson Co.
Madison Heights, MI

The annual meeting of a major automobile manufacturer, introducing its new models, is always a big production, and Mitsubishi's session, scheduled for April 1991, was a specially big one. But just 68 days prior to that date, it was shifted from Tokyo to Dallas, due to the dangers of the Gulf War.

The available space was a big barn of a room, with very many columns. But a clever floor plan made the room manageable, and the few columns that remained were less conspicuous when surrounded by circular food-serving tables.

EXHIBITOR
Ducks Unlimited
DESIGNER
R. Marvin Cook, Jr.
PRODUCER
Wilderness Graphics Inc.
Tallahassee, FL

The flexibility of the design permits its use in a variety of settings, running from appearance at a trade show to a civic event. The array of components, which can be displayed in a variety of configurations, all fits into a 6 × 12′ customized trailer.

EXHIBITOR
Mary Kay Cosmetics
DESIGNER
Jim Baridon
PRODUCER
Freeman Exhibit Co.
Dallas, TX

Designed for the main lobby of the exhibitor's company headquarters, these well lit cabinets display products attractively, but their placing does not interfere with traffic flow.

CHAPTER

MUSEUM EXHIBITS

EXHIBITOR
National Lacrosse Foundation
DESIGNER
Ronald Adler, Elizabeth Lockett
PRODUCER
Adler Display Inc.
Baltimore, MD

The Lacrosse Hall of Fame Museum, located on the Johns Hopkins campus in Baltimore, contains a time-line of the history of lacrosse from the 1600s to the present, a Hall of Fame exhibit, a trophy exhibit, and a gift shop.

EXHIBITOR
Technology Center of Silicon Valley
DESIGNER
A + O STUDIO San Francisco
PRODUCER
F.W. Dixon
Woburn, MA

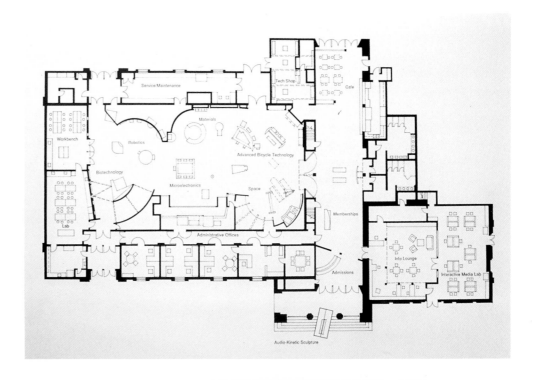

This project involved the development, design, and installation of a brand new museum in an existing building, completely renovated for this purpose. The focus of the interim museum, occupying 17,000 square feet, is current technology, especially what it means to today's students.

With limited funding, the design team had to be very selective about architectural elements and the combinations of materials and detailing. Sheet linoleum took on new light as wainscotting and exhibit surfaces, for example. Each of the topic areas includes interactive exhibits.

EXHIBITOR
National Aquarium
Baltimore, MD
DESIGNER
Lorena Streb, Gary Ebersole
PRODUCER
Adler Display Inc.
Baltimore, MD

To celebrate its 10th anniversary, the aquarium used this hallway display, celebrating the decade with photos, publications and posters.

EXHIBITOR
Julian Stanley Wise Foundation, Virginia
Association of Volunteer Rescue Squads
DESIGNER
Ed Krent, Trisha Hanlon
PRODUCER
Julian Stanley Wise Foundation

This museum, the first devoted to
volunteer life saving and rescue
squads, uses interactive media and
role-playing to capture the drama
of rescue efforts. Unique historical
equipment is juxtaposed with mod-
ern equipment to emphasize recent
technological advances.

EXHIBITOR
Maryland Geological Survey
DESIGNER
David McLean, David McLean Assoc.
PRODUCER
Adler Display Inc.
Baltimore, MD

The Sideling Hill Interpretive Center is a permanent exhibit in western Maryland, taking advantage of a 380′ vertical cut into the hill during the construction of Interstate Highway 68. The exhibits explain the geological significance of the exposed rock, as well as serving as a general introduction to geology.

EXHIBITOR
National Civil Rights Museum
Memphis, TN
DESIGNER
Gerard Eisterhold, Eisterhold Associates
PRODUCER
Design & Production
Lorton, VA

Located at the Lorraine Motel, in
Memphis, where Martin Luther
King, Jr. had been assassinated,
this museum traces the history of
the struggle for civil rights, using
life-size, abstract mannequins,
video clips, reconstructions, and
artifacts, to bring a dramatic story
to life.

CONTINUED

CONTINUED

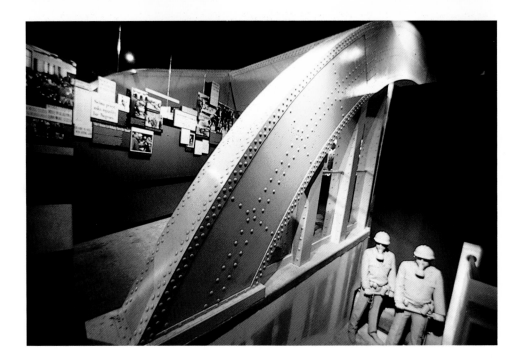

EXHIBITOR
World Trade Center
DESIGNER
Mark Holme
PRODUCER
Giltspur/Boston
Avon, MA

In addition to 15 animated dinosaurs in realistic environments, the exhibit includes two theaters, a display of fossils, some interactive displays, a storyteller, and a gift shop.

CONTINUED

EXHIBITOR
Cincinnati Historical Society
DESIGNER
Clark Swayze, J. Patrick Mason, Janet Danek
PRODUCER
Design Craftsmen Inc.
Midland, MI

"Cincinnati Goes to War: A Community's Response to World War II" brings this dramatic period to life through the use of audio-visual and interactive programs, period environments and an exceptional collection of photographs and artifacts. The environments are enhanced by the use of 15 cast figures. These poignant, monochromatic statues add human drama to the space. There are eight special audio or visual displays, as well as a scrap drive truck being loaded, a factory, an enlistment office, and an interactive celebration of VE Day.

CONTINUED

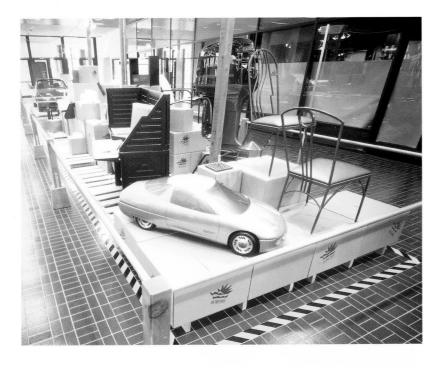

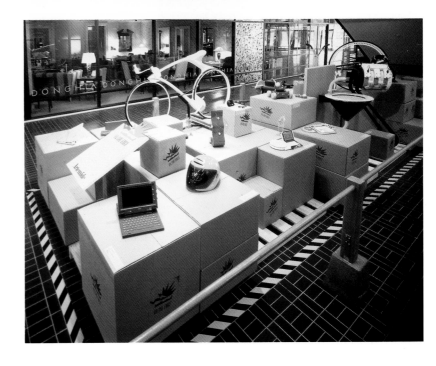

EXHIBITOR
IDSA/LA
DESIGNER/PRODUCER
Industrial Designers Society of America
Southern California Chapter

Opened during WestWeek at the
Pacific Design Center, Los Angeles,
this exhibit showcases industrial
design. Products were presented
not as museum pieces, but rather
as items found in our daily lives.
The exhibit atmosphere was like an
active warehouse in which products were being packaged for
shipment across the country.

EXHIBITOR
World Trade Center
DESIGNER
Mark Holme
PRODUCER
Giltspur/Boston
Avon, MA

In addition to 15 animated dinosaurs in realistic environments, the exhibit includes two theaters, a display of fossils, some interactive displays, a storyteller, and a gift shop.

CONTINUED

193

CONTINUED

EXHIBITOR
Missouri Botanical Garden
DESIGNER
Krent/Paffett Associates Inc.
Boston, MA
PRODUCER
Museum Services
Gainesville, FL

Within a geodesic dome at the Botanical Garden is a living example of a tropical rain forest. The exhibits and their interpretive signs must be able to resist the high humidity and temperature expected in that part of the world.

CONTINUED

201

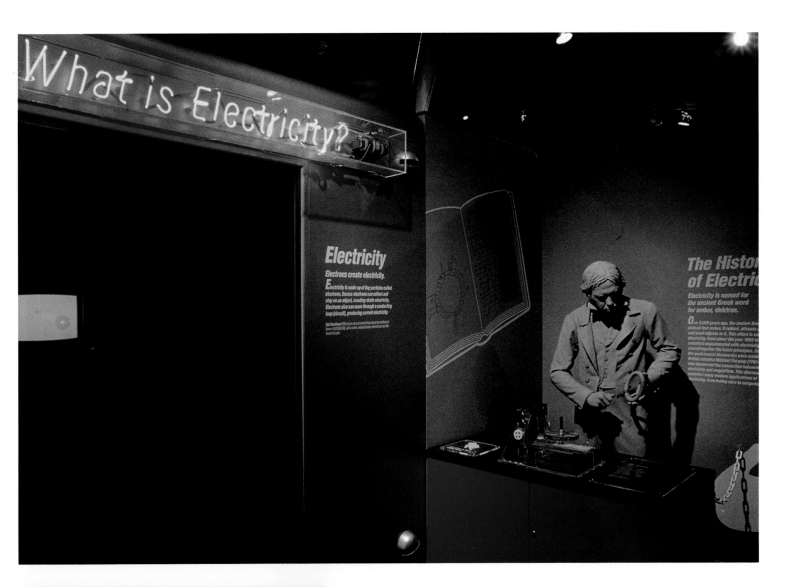

EXHIBITOR
Discovery Museum
DESIGNER
Krent/Paffett Associates Inc.
Boston, MA
PRODUCER
Rathe Productions
New York, NY

Science and art are the two creative disciplines that are accessible in this interactive gallery, located in Bridgeport, Connecticut, where adults and children are invited to experiment, create, and perform. Many interactive devices permit visitors to learn by doing.

CONTINUED

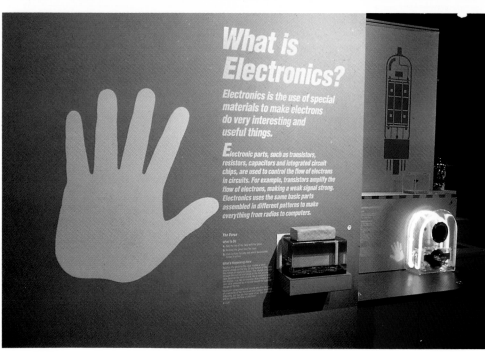

EXHIBITOR
Naval Undersea Museum
DESIGNER
Alan Ransenberg
PRODUCER
Promotion Products Inc.
Portland, OR

This highly specialized exhibit on natural science and the technological development of the underseas uses brightly-lit panels in a dimly-lit room.

EXHIBITOR
Indiana Michigan Power
DESIGNER/PRODUCER
Lester Associates Inc.
West Nyack, NY

This automated newsroom of the
21st century was developed for the
Cook Energy Information Center, at
Bridgman, Michigan. Android news-
casters were animated to match a
recorded sound track, as pictures
were shown on the three 35″
screens. Another camera integrates
the audience into each show, showing them on the monitors before
the formal presentation begins.

EXHIBITOR
Chick-fil-A Corp.
DESIGNER
Jeffrey Raflo
PRODUCER
Murphy & Orr Exhibits
Forest Park, GA

Here is a replica of the first grill
opened by the company, in 1946. A
9′6″ high wall displays life-size
transparencies of the grill's neighborhood when it first opened. A
fully restored 1946 Ford and a
model Delta plane overhead recog-
nize the importance of the proximity of the Atlanta Airport and a
Ford plant to the success of the
company. Display cases show artifacts of the period.

EXHIBITOR
St. Vincent National Wildlife Refuge
DESIGNER
R. Marvin Cook, Jr.
PRODUCER
Wilderness Graphics Inc.
Tallahassee, FL

Among the exhibits at the visitor center of the off-shore St. Vincent National Refuge at Apalichicola, Florida, is a diorama which shows a pair of ospreys at their nest and an adult red wolf, an endangered species. There is also a relief model that relates the island to the larger estuarine system.

EXHIBITOR
Lorain County Metropolitan Park District
DESIGNER
R. Marvin Cook, Jr.
PRODUCER
Wilderness Graphics Inc.
Tallahassee, FL

Designed with children in mind, these exhibits are straightforward and simple. One end of a tree is used to show the value of a dead tree in the forest, while the other end relates the tree and its rings to history. Other techniques include secret doors, cube puzzles, and touchscreen computer games.

EXHIBITOR
Historic Spanish Point Packing House
DESIGNER
R. Marvin Cook, Jr.
PRODUCER
Wilderness Graphics Inc.
Tallahassee, FL

Exhibits, designed to demonstrate how a turn-of-the-century packing house operated, are reproductions of actual packing house equipment. Interpretive panels describe the operation.

EXHIBITOR
Museum of Natural History of Florida Keys
DESIGNER
R. Marvin Cook, Jr.
PRODUCER
Wilderness Graphics Inc.
Tallahassee, FL

Visitors can dive 30' underwater—without getting wet—when they pass through the replica of a coral reef cave. A glimpse of the reef, complete with shark, sea turtle, ray, and other denizens of the deep, can be viewed from US Highway 1.

213

EXHIBITOR
New York Transit Museum
DESIGNER/PRODUCER
Structural Display Inc.
Long Island City, NY

This museum was installed in an actual subway station, closed many years ago. The space has been converted into a museum exhibition of the complete history of this public transportation system.

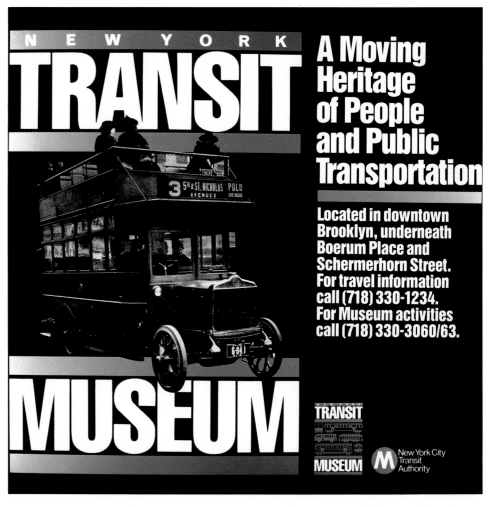

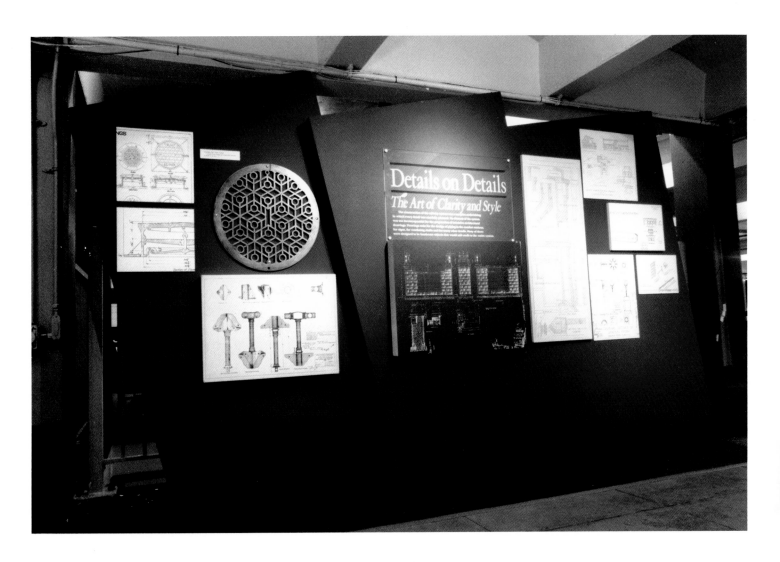

The Astor Place Kiosk

A Bit of Budapest

Heins & LaFarge were also responsible for all above ground architectural features related to the stations. Their most famous design was that of the cast-iron and wire glass kiosks that once protected the entrances to the stations. These kiosks were modeled after those in use on the Budapest subway system. A single kiosk was reconstructed at Astor Place during the restoration of that station in the mid 1980s. As part of the restoration, architect Rolf Ohlhausen used photographs that he had taken of the original kiosk while a student at Cooper Union in the early 1950s to recreate the original. The cast-iron kiosk was manufactured at the Robinson Ironworks in Birmingham, Alabama.

EXHIBITOR
Carnegie Science Center
DESIGNER
Krent/Paffett Associates Inc.
Boston, MA
PRODUCER
Giltspur/Pittsburgh
Pittsburgh, PA

Science Way is the introductory gallery of the new Carnegie Science Center in Pittsburgh. Its focus is on how scientists work and think. A collection of about 30 interactive exhibits interprets basic procedures—observing and collecting data, building and testing models, developing and testing hypotheses, and applying new ideas to the world.

Physically, the gallery is patterned after a small neighborhood, somewhere between the recognizable streets of Pittsburgh and the fertile world of the scientist's imagination.

CONTINUED

EXHIBITOR
Pacific Science Center
DESIGNER
Daniel Quan, David Taylor, Pacific Science
Center
PRODUCER
Pacific Science Center
Seattle, WA

This traveling exhibit, about 8,000 square feet, used animated models of five different species of whales, about 85 percent full-scale. Visitors enter the exhibit via a dark, narrow cave which opens out into a cavernous "undersea" space, where they first face a sperm whale chasing a squid. Other whales are revealed as the visitor moves between rocks, kelp, and undersea arches.

Interspersed among the rocks are interactive games, informational graphics, and "Passport" stamping stations, as well as more traditional displays. There is also a small video theater, a "tots" area, and a Whales Store.

CONTINUED

EXHIBITOR
Science Place
DESIGNER/PRODUCER
Rogow + Bernstein
Los Angeles, CA

This comprehensive gallery, in Dallas, is intended to interest young people in the nature of physics. Most of the exhibits are hands-on, some at a "gee whiz" level for small children, others designed to reach gifted fifth-graders, and still others that re-quire a knowledge of high school algebra.

VISCOUS LIQUIDS

TURN THE WHEEL UNTIL THE TUBES ARE UPSIDE DOWN. OBJECTS SINK AND BUBBLES RISE MORE SLOWLY IN SOME LIQUIDS THAN IN OTHERS.

All liquids resist flow, some more than others. Resistance to flow is the liquid's vis-cosity. The more viscous the liquid, the more slowly objects and bubbles travel through it.

The attraction of a liquid's molecules for one another determines its viscosity. A stronger attraction means greater viscosity.

Liquids have characteristic viscosities. Maple syrup is less viscous than molasses and more viscous than water, for example.

Furthermore, warm molasses flows faster because higher temperatures tend to decrease viscosity of liquids. As a liquid warms, its molecules increasingly jostle each other. This force counteracts the attraction among the liquid's molecules, reducing viscosity. The opposite occurs when a liquid cools.

EXHIBITOR
Herbert H. Dow Historical Museum
DESIGNER
Janet Danek, J. Patrick Mason
PRODUCER
Design Craftsmen Inc.
Midland, MI

The museum was created to commemorate the accomplishments of Herbert Henry Dow, the founder of the Dow Chemical Company, as well as delving into his personality. The displays include a replica of the mill where Mr. Dow started the operation, his father's workshop, his mother's kitchen, and his first office.

The final environment features four cast figures seated around a table, in animated discussion. An audio program provides background on the individuals who formed the company. Two other visual presentations outline the contributions of the company to chemistry and to the community of Midland.

EXHIBITOR
National Museum of American History
DESIGNER
Rogow + Bernstein
PRODUCER
National Museum of American History
Washington, D.C.

This installation, in the Smithsonian Institution, occupies some 12,000 square feet. Entitled "Information Age: People, Information & Technology," the show includes some 700 objects and artifacts, ranging from Morse's telegraph to an early Apple computer.
There are many interactive experiences and demonstrations.

CONTINUED

CONTINUED

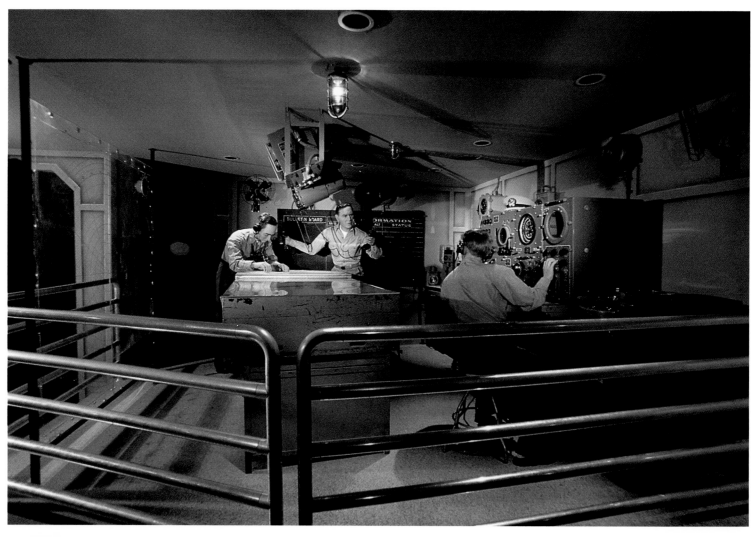

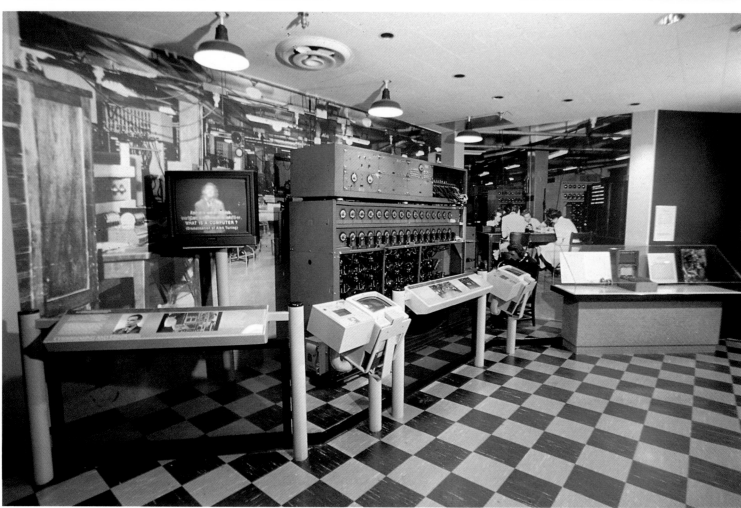

Appendix

A + O Studio
1131 Tennessee St.
San Francisco, CA 94107

Accent Exhibits Designs & Displays
2560 Madison Ave.
Baltimore, MD 21217

Ad-Ex International
895 Glendale-Milford Rd.
Cincinnati, OH 45215

Adler Display Inc.
1101 E. 25th St.
Baltimore, MD 21218

All West Display
2337 N. W. York
Portland, OR 97210

Beitel Displays & Exhibits Inc.
1880 Princeton Ave.
Lawrenceville, NJ 08648

Bill Warfel & Associates
22500 West Edgewood Ave.
Big Bend, WI 53103

Bluepeter
555 Illinois St.
San Francisco, CA 94017

Boss Display Corp.
1585 Frebis Lane
Columbus, OH 43206

CES
429 North Prior Ave.
Saint Paul, MN 55104

Color & Design Exhibits Inc.
3625 N. Mississippi Ave.
Portland, OR 97227

Communication Exhibits Inc.
239 N. Canal St.
Canal Fulton, OH 44614

Convention Exhibits
2221 S. Michigan Ave.
Chicago, IL 60626-2188

Daniel Burk Designs Inc.
2513 Hargrave Dr.
Los Angeles, CA 90068

Dell Displays Inc.
2701 United Lane
Elk Grove Village, IL 60007

Denby Associates
P.O. Box 3772
Princeton, NJ 08543

The Derse Company
1234 N. 62 St.
Milwaukee, WI 53212-0555

Design & Production
7110 Rainwater Place
Lorton, VA 22079

Design Craftsmen Inc.
2200 James Savage Rd.
Midland, MI 48641-2126

Design Fabrication
1090 Wheaton St.
Troy, MI 48084

Design South
3655 Atlanta Ind Dr. #100
Atlanta, GA 30331

Designer's Workshop
3860 Green Industrial Way
Chamblee, GA 30314

Dimensional Studios Inc.
120 E. Ninth Ave.
Runnemede, NJ 08078

Display Center Showroom
8459 E. Castlewood Dr.
Indiannapolis, IN 46250

Echelon Design Inc.
2340 S. Arlington Heights Rd.
Arlington Heights, IL 60005

Eisterhold Associates
218 Delaware #111
Kansas City, MO 69105

Ernest F. Ambrosius & Sohn; Fairconsult
Bismarckstrasse 12
5000 Koln 1/Germany

Everbrite Inc.
4949 S. 110 St.
Greenfield, WI 53220

Exhibit Bilders Inc.
9119 Carpenter Freeway
Dallas, TX 75247

Exhibit Builders Inc.
1526 W. 25th St.
Cleveland, OH 44113

Exhibit by Design
3255 N. Arlington Heights Rd.
Arlington Heights, IL 60004

Exhibitgroup
100 Utah Ave.
San Francisco, CA 94080

Exhibitgroup Atlanta
180 Selig Dr.
Atlanta, GA 30336

Exhibitgroup San Francisco
100 Utah Ave.
South San Francisco, CA 94080

Exhibit Technology Inc.
70 James St.
Worcester, MA 01603

Exhibitree Inc.
9700 Toledo Way
Irvine, CA 92718

FM Productions
3775 Bay Shore Blvd.
Brisbane, CA 94005

Freeman Exhibit Co.
8301 Ambassador Row
Dallas, TX 74247-4726

F.W. Dixon
55 Salem St.
Woburn, MA 01801

General Exhibits Inc.
2038 Washington Ave.
Philadelphia, PA 19146

George P. Johnson Co.
800 Tech Row
Madison Heights, MI 48071

Giltspur/Boston
175 Bodwell St.
Avon, MA 02322

Giltspur/Chicago
3225 S. Western Ave.
Chicago, IL 60608-6091

Giltspur/Pittsburgh
P.O. Box 1000
Pittsburgh, PA 15230-1000

Giltspur/Rochester
1143 Lexington Ave.
Rochester, NY 14606

Graphics 55
55 Avondale Ave.
Clifton, NJ 07013

Haas Exhibit Marketing
7125 Sandburg Rd.
Minneapolis, MN 55427

Hartwig Exhibitions
1325 N. Van Buren St.
Milwaukee, WI 53202

C. Henning Studios
549 Amsterdam Ave.
Atlanta, GA 30306

Heritage Display Group/Dallas
800 Cadiz St.
Dallas, TX 75215

Howard Displays Inc.
2361 S. State St.
Chicago, IL 60616

IDSA/LA
24009 Ventura Blvd. #200
Calbass, CA 91302

i e Design
1088 Irvine Blvd. #330
Tustin, CA 92680

John Oldham Studios Inc.
888 Wells Rd.
Wethersfield, CT 06109

Julian Stanley Wise Foundation
Box 1904
Roanoke, VA 24008

Kitzing Inc.
1323 W. Carroll Ave.
Chicago, IL 60607

Krent/Paffet Associates Inc.
711 Atlantic Ave.
Boston, MA 02111

Laarhoven Design Inc.
1790 Corporate Dr.
Norcross, GA 30093

Lester Associates Inc.
103 N. Route 303
West Nyack, NY 10994

Loreno Design
3475 Lenox Rd. NE #460
Atlanta, GA 30326

L.W. Milby Inc. Exhibits
1701 Dalton Dr.
New Carslisle, OH 45344

Mauk Design
636 Fourth Street
San Francisco, CA 94117

McMillan Group
523 Danbury Rd.
Wilton, CT 06897

Mount Vernon Displays Inc.
316 N. 8th St.
Prospect Park, NJ 07508

Murphy & Orr Exhibits
564 Main St.
Forest Park, GA 30050

Museum Services
1220 S.E. Veitch St.
Gainsville, FL 32601

Nomadic Display
7400 Fullerton Rd. #154
Springfield, VA 22153

Pacific Science Center
200 Second Avenue North
Seattle, WA 98109

Pingel Displays Inc.
2655 Victor St.
St. Louis, MO 63104

Promotional Fixtures Inc.
40 Industrial St.
Rittman, OH 44270

Promotion Products Inc.
50 S.E. Yamhill St.
Portland, OR 97201

Rathe Productions
555 W. 23rd St.
New York, NY 10011

The Robert Falk Group
4425 West Pine
St. Louis, MO 63108

Rogers Display Co.
7550 Tyler Blvd.
Mentor, OH 44060

Rogow & Bernstein
5971 West Third St.
Los Angeles, CA 90036

Scotia Woodworking
95 Grand St.
Worcester, MA 01610

Skyline Displays Inc.
12345 Portland Ave. S.
Burnsville, MN 55337

Stevens Exhibits/Display Inc.
3900 S. Union Ave.
Chicago, IL 60609

Structural Display Inc.
12-12 33rd Ave.
Long Island City, NY 11106

TW Design & Construction
4731 Algiers St.
Dallas, TX 75201

United Longchamp International
1650-A Claudina Way
Anaheim, CA 92805

United Longchamp International
953 Donnelly S.W. Ave.
Atlanta, GA 30310

United Longchamp International
1313 S. Michigan Ave.
Chicago, IL 60605

W.E. Murphy & Co. Chicago
2023 West Carroll Ave.
Chicago, IL 60612

Wilderness Graphics Inc.
324-g W. Van Buren St.
Tallahassee, FL 32301

Index

EXHIBITORS

DESIGNERS

PRODUCERS